INSECTS STICKER BOOK

Anthony Wootton
Illustrated by Phil Weare

Edited by Phillip Clarke
Designed by Leonard Le Rolland
Consultant: Margaret Rostron

How to use this book

An insect is a small animal with a body divided into three main parts, and six legs. Most insects have wings. There are more than a hundred insects in this book. Using the descriptions and pictures, match each insect sticker to the right description. If you need help, an index and checklist at the back of the book tells you where the sticker should go. You can also use this book as a spotter's handbook to make a note of the insects you have seen.

Here are some of the words used to describe insects:

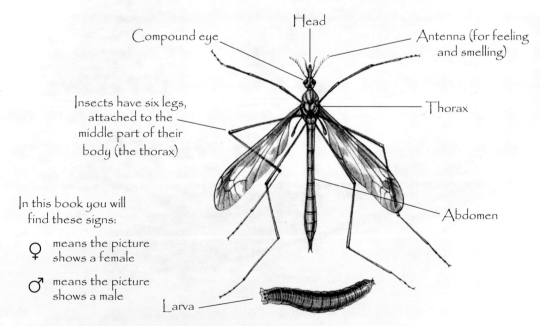

Compound eye

Head

Antenna (for feeling and smelling)

Insects have six legs, attached to the middle part of their body (the thorax)

Thorax

Abdomen

In this book you will find these signs:

♀ means the picture shows a female

♂ means the picture shows a male

Larva

Many insects have young called larvae, that look totally different from the adults. The name for one is a larva. Butterfly and moth larvae are called caterpillars. Other insects have young called nymphs that look like small, wingless adults.

Butterflies

Wall brown

Wall brown

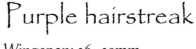

Wingspan: 44–46mm

This brown butterfly has spots that look like eyes on its front and back wings. It is often found in dry, open spaces.

WHEN ....

WHERE ....

Brown argus

Brown argus

Wingspan: 28–30mm

This butterfly has brown wings with orange marks near the edges. You may spot it on chalky downs in southern England or Wales. The males are said to smell of chocolate when they are trying to attract females.

WHEN ....

WHERE ....

Clouded yellow

Clouded yellow

Wingspan: 58–62mm

Clouded yellows have pale orange wings with dark edges. They fly to Britain from southern Europe in the spring.

WHEN ....

WHERE ....

Purple hairstreak

Wingspan: 36–39mm

Purple hairstreaks fly around the tops of oak trees. Males have purplish wings with black borders. Females have black wings with purplish streaks on the front wings.

WHEN ....

WHERE ....

Purple hairstreak

Marbled white

Wingspan: 53–58mm

Marbled whites have marbled black and white wings. They are found all over Europe, and are common in southern England.

WHEN ....

WHERE ....

Marbled white

Brimstone

♂

Brimstone

Wingspan: 58–62mm

This large, yellow butterfly is not found in Scotland, but is common in the rest of Britain. The female is pale greenish white.

WHEN ....

WHERE ....

Small tortoiseshell

Wingspan: 50–56mm

Common throughout the UK, this butterfly has brightly patterned wings with blue half-moons along the edges.

WHEN ....

WHERE ....

Small
tortoiseshell

Peacock

Peacock

Wingspan: 62–68mm

Adult peacocks hibernate in the winter. Their large wings are brightly coloured with eye-like markings.

WHEN ....

WHERE ....

♀

Cabbage white

Pearl-bordered fritillary

Wingspan: 42–46mm

Pearl-bordered fritillaries have black markings on their orange-brown wings, and pearly spots underneath. They can be found all over Britain.

WHEN ....

WHERE ....

Pearl-bordered fritillary

Cabbage white

Wingspan: 48–50mm

You might see this common white butterfly flitting around gardens, especially near cabbages.

WHEN ....

WHERE ....

3

Moths

Lobster moth

Puss moth

Puss moth

Wingspan: 65–80mm

Found commonly
throughout Britain, puss
moths are pale pink and grey.
When their caterpillars are alarmed,
thin red "whips" stick out of their tails.

WHEN ....

WHERE ....

Caterpillar

Emperor moth

♀

Emperor moth

Wingspan: Female 70mm
Male 55mm

Emperor moths have yellowish, eye-
like wing spots. Females are grey
and white. Males are smaller, with
a more reddish tinge, orange back
wings and more feathery antennae.

WHEN ....

WHERE ....

Lobster moth

Wingspan: 65–70mm

This moth gets its name from
its caterpillar's tail end, which
looks like a lobster's claw. The
adult is a dull, grey-brown colour.

WHEN ....

WHERE ....

Claw-like
tail

Hummingbird
hawk-moth

Hummingbird
hawk-moth

Wingspan: 45mm

You might see this little moth hovering over
flowers and beating its wings like a hummingbird.
It has brown front wings and orange back wings.

WHEN ....

WHERE ....

Peach blossom

Peach blossom

Wingspan: 35mm

Peach blossoms can be found
in woodland. They take their
name from the pink spots on
their brown front wings.

WHEN ....

WHERE ....

Clifden nonpareil or blue underwing

Wingspan: 90mm

This moth is rare, but you might come across it in eastern or southern England. It has mottled grey front wings and dark back wings with pale blue stripes around them.

WHEN ....

WHERE ....

Clifden nonpareil

Red underwing

Red underwing

Wingspan: 80mm

When birds threaten it, this moth flashes its red and black back wings. The colour of its front wings matches the bark of trees.

WHEN ....

WHERE ....

♂ Vapourer

Silver Y

Wingspan: 40mm

A silver Y is a dull-coloured moth, with white markings on its front wings shaped like the letter "Y".

WHEN ....

WHERE ....

Vapourer

Wingspan: 35mm

Male vapourers have brown wings, but females only have wing stubs so they can't fly. Vapourers can be found all over Britain.

WHEN ....

WHERE ....

♀

Caterpillar

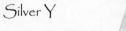
Silver Y

Oak eggar

Wingspan: 50–65mm

Oak eggars have brown wings with yellow edges and a white spot on each front wing. The male has feather-like antennae.

WHEN ....

WHERE ....

Oak eggar
♂

Moths

Garden tiger

Wingspan: 60–70mm

Garden tigers have orange back wings with black spots. Their front wings are mottled brown and cream. This moth's caterpillar is called a woolly bear.

WHEN ....

WHERE ....

Garden tiger

Woolly bear

Ghost moth

Wingspan: 50–60mm

Female ghost moths have browner wings than the white males, and so are better camouflaged.

WHEN ....

WHERE ....

Ghost moth

♂

Wood tiger

Wingspan: 35–40mm

Look in open woodland, and on hillsides and heaths, for this brown and cream patterned moth.

WHEN ....

WHERE ....

Wood tiger

Lappet moth

Wingspan: 60–70mm

Lappet moths hold their veined brown wings so that they overlap, making them look like bunches of dry leaves. Their caterpillars have flaps called lappets along their sides.

WHEN ....

WHERE ....

Lappet moth

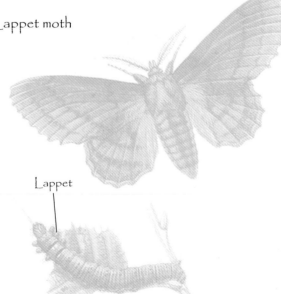

Lappet

Swallow-tailed moth

Wingspan: 56mm

This pale-coloured moth has large petal-shaped wings which make it look like a butterfly. It flies in a weak, fluttering way.

WHEN ....

WHERE ....

Swallow-tailed moth

Death's head hawk-moth

Wingspan: 100–125mm

The skull-like markings on its thorax give this rare moth its grisly name. Its front wings are patterned brown and its back wings are light brown with darker stripes. Death's head hawk-moths lay their eggs on potato leaves.

WHEN ....

WHERE ....

Death's head hawk-moth

Cinnabar

Ragwort

Cinnabar

Wingspan: 40–45mm

You might see this moth flying short distances by day. It has red back wings and dark brown front wings marked with two spots and two red streaks. Its yellow and black caterpillars can be seen on ragwort.

WHEN ....

WHERE ....

Six-spot burnet

Wingspan: 35mm

Six-spot burnets take their name from the six red spots on each of their brown front wings. Their back wings are red, and their bright colour warns birds that they taste bad.

WHEN ....

WHERE ....

Six-spot burnet

Eyed hawk-moth

Forester

Wingspan: 25–27mm

This little moth has green front wings and pale back wings. It can often be seen flying over meadows in the summer.

WHEN ....

WHERE ....

Forester

Eyed hawk-moth

Wingspan: 75–80mm

These moths have large eye-like markings on their pink and brown back wings. They show them quickly to frighten off their enemies.

WHEN ....

WHERE ....

Beetles

Seven-spot ladybird

Length: 6–7mm

These red ladybirds, with their seven black spots, are very common in Britain. You're most likely to see them on sunny days.

WHEN ....

WHERE ....

Seven-spot ladybird

Rose chafer

Length: 14–20mm

A rose chafer's wing cases look almost square, but the front of its thorax is very round. This green beetle can be found all over Britain.

WHEN ....

WHERE ....

Rose chafer

Cockchafer or maybug

Length: 25–30mm

You might see this beetle flying into lit windows in the early summer. It has a black head, brown wing cases, and is furry underneath its thorax.

WHEN ....

WHERE ....

Cockchafer

Musk beetle

Musk beetle

Length: 20–32mm

This beetle has a very long, green body and even longer beady antennae.

WHEN ....

WHERE ....

Water beetle

Water beetle

Length: 7–8mm

Water beetles are common in lakes and rivers. Their colour varies from brown to black. They lay their eggs on water plants.

WHEN ....

WHERE ....

Stag beetle

♂

Stag beetle

Length: 25–75mm

The largest beetles in Britain, male stag beetles have purplish wing cases, a black head and legs and long, antler-like jaws.

WHEN ....

WHERE ....

Cardinal beetle

Length: 15–17mm

There are three kinds of cardinal beetle in Europe. This one has a long, red body, and antennae with branches along them. It can be found on flowers and under bark.

WHEN ....

WHERE ....

Cardinal beetle

Green tiger beetle

Length: 12–15mm

A fierce, sharp-jawed hunter, this common beetle is seen in open woodlands and sandy areas in early summer. The larvae make burrows, and lie in wait to ambush ants.

WHEN ....

WHERE ....

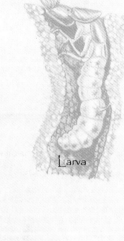

Larva

Click beetle or skip-jack

Length: 14–18mm

If these beetles fall onto their backs they flip their bodies into the air with a loud click. There are many types: this one has a sleek, green body and branched antennae. Its larva is called a wireworm.

WHEN ....

WHERE ....

Click beetle

Green tiger beetle

Wireworm

Glow-worm

Male length: 15mm
Female length: 20mm

Female glow-worms have long, brown bodies without wings or wing-cases. They attract males with their glowing tails.

WHEN ....

WHERE ....

Great diving beetle

Length: 30–35mm

Great diving beetles live in lakes and ponds. Their bodies are black with light brown edges, and they have brown legs and antennae.

WHEN ....

WHERE ....

Great diving beetle

Larva

♀

Larva

♂

Glow-worm

Beetles

Wasp beetle

Length: 15mm

This beetle looks like a wasp, with yellow stripes along its brown body. It flies around flowers on sunny days.

WHEN ....

WHERE ....

Wasp beetle

Colorado beetle

Length: 10–12mm

You should tell the police if you spot one of these beetles, as they damage potato crops. You can recognize a Colorado beetle by its rounded body and the dark and light brown stripes along its wing cases.

WHEN ....

WHERE ....

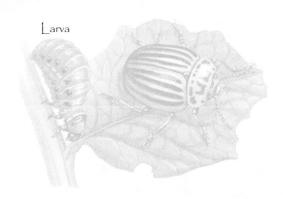

Larva

Colorado beetle

Bloody-nosed beetle

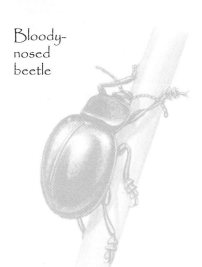

Bloody-nosed beetle

Length: 10–20mm

If this beetle is threatened, it produces a smelly red liquid from its mouth. The leaf-eating beetle has round, black wing cases which are joined together, so it can't fly.

WHEN ....

WHERE ....

Green tortoise beetle

Length: 6–8mm

When their legs and antennae are hidden, these round beetles look a bit like little tortoises. The spiny larvae put off hungry enemies by carrying their own droppings and dead skins in their forked tails.

WHEN ....

WHERE ....

Nut weevil

Length: 10mm

Female nut weevils have very long snouts and rounded, brown bodies. They use their snouts (called rostrums) to make holes in young hazelnuts, where they lay a single egg. The larva then grows inside the nut, eating the kernel.

WHEN ....

WHERE ....

Nut weevil

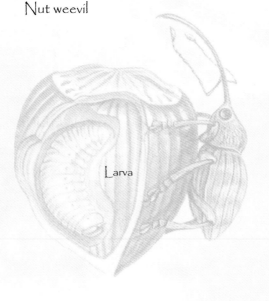

Larva

Green tortoise beetle

Larva

Devil's coach horse or cocktail beetle

Length: 25–30mm

Often found in gardens, this black beetle can squirt a foul-smelling liquid from its tail at its enemies.

WHEN ....

WHERE ....

Devil's coach horse

Great silver water beetle

Length: 37–48mm

The largest water beetle in Britain, this has a large, black body with hairy back legs, and claws on its front legs.

WHEN ....

WHERE ....

Great silver water beetle

Rove beetle

Length: 20mm

There are different kinds of rove beetle. This one has red eyes and legs, a red section in the thorax and a long, black tail. Rove beetles eat dead animals.

WHEN ....

WHERE ....

Horned dung beetle or minotaur beetle

Length: 12–18mm

This black beetle has broad, ribbed wing cases, tough, thick legs and large horns around its head.

WHEN ....

WHERE ....

Horned dung beetle

Death watch beetle

Length: 7–10mm

The ticking noise this beetle makes as it tunnels through wood, knocking its head on the walls, was once thought to mean that someone was about to die. It eats the wood in damp timber buildings, such as old barns. Death watch beetles are mottled dark and light brown.

WHEN ....

WHERE ....

Death watch beetle

Rove beetle

Bugs

Water boatman or backswimmer

Length: 15mm

A water boatman's brown body is rather like a little boat. It swims on its back, with the tips of its legs clinging to the underside of the water surface. Its back legs are shaped like paddles and fringed with hairs.

WHEN ....

WHERE ....

Water boatman

Water cricket

Length: 6–7mm

Water crickets have long legs and dark bodies with two light brown stripes along them. You can find them on the surface of still water, eating insects and spiders.

WHEN ....

WHERE ....

Water cricket

Saucer bug

Length: 12–16mm

This bug lives among plants at the bottom of muddy pools and canals. It has short legs, and the front ones are rounded and very sharp. Beware of their sharp, stabbing jaws.

WHEN ....

WHERE ....

Saucer bug

Pond skater

Length: 8–10mm

Pond skaters are small, with very long legs and thin bodies. They skate with their middle legs, use their back legs as rudders and their front legs to catch prey.

WHEN ....

WHERE ....

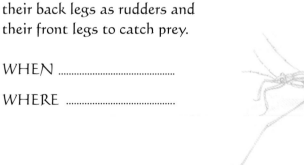

Pond skater

Black and red froghopper

Length: 9–10mm

When it is disturbed, this red and black striped bug jumps. Most froghopper nymphs produce globs of froth, known as cuckoo-spit.

WHEN ....

WHERE ....

Black and red froghopper

1

2

3

5

4

6

7

8

Ovipositor

♀

9

10

11

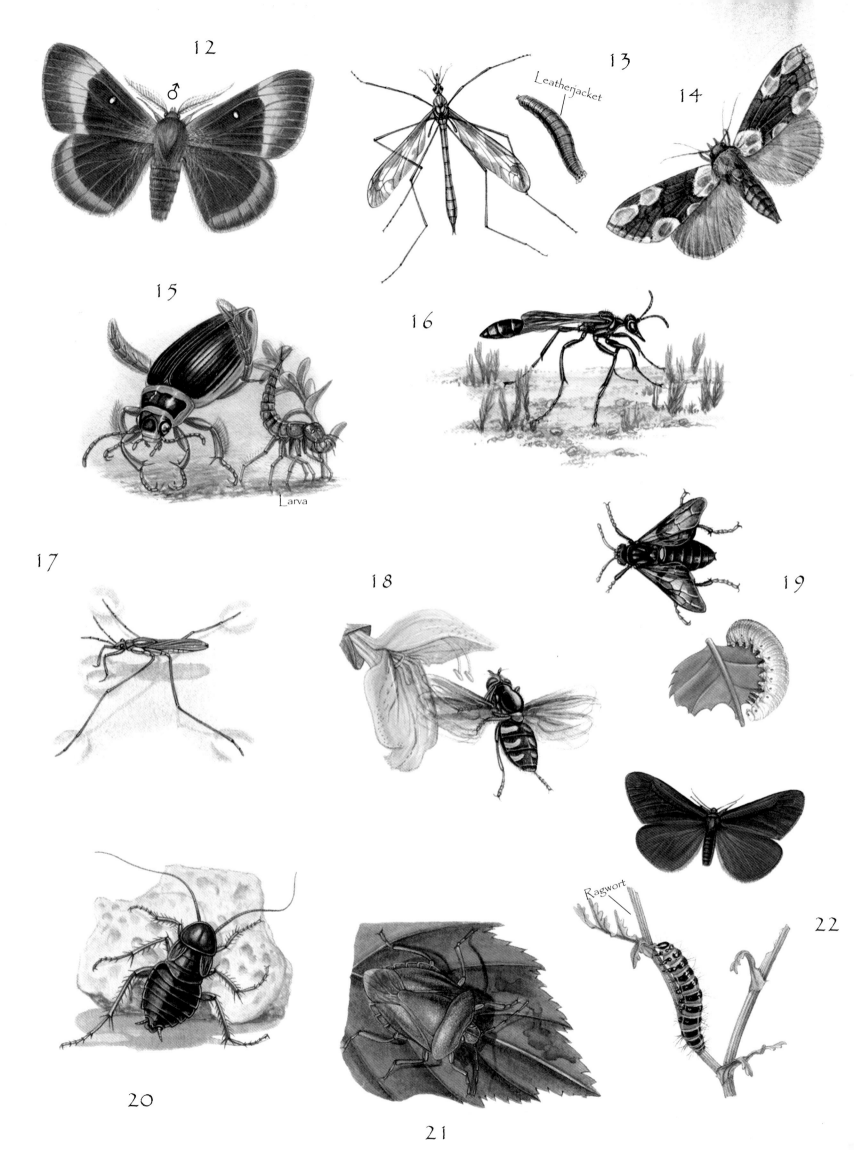

12

13

Leatherjacket

14

15

16

17

18

19

Larva

20

21

22

Ragwort

23

24

Wireworm

25 ♂

26

27 ♂ Curly tail ♀

28 ♂

29 Marble gall

30

31 ♀

32 ♂

33 Larva

34

35

36

37

Caterpillar

38 ♂

39

40 Pot

41

42

43

44 ♂

♀

Caterpillar

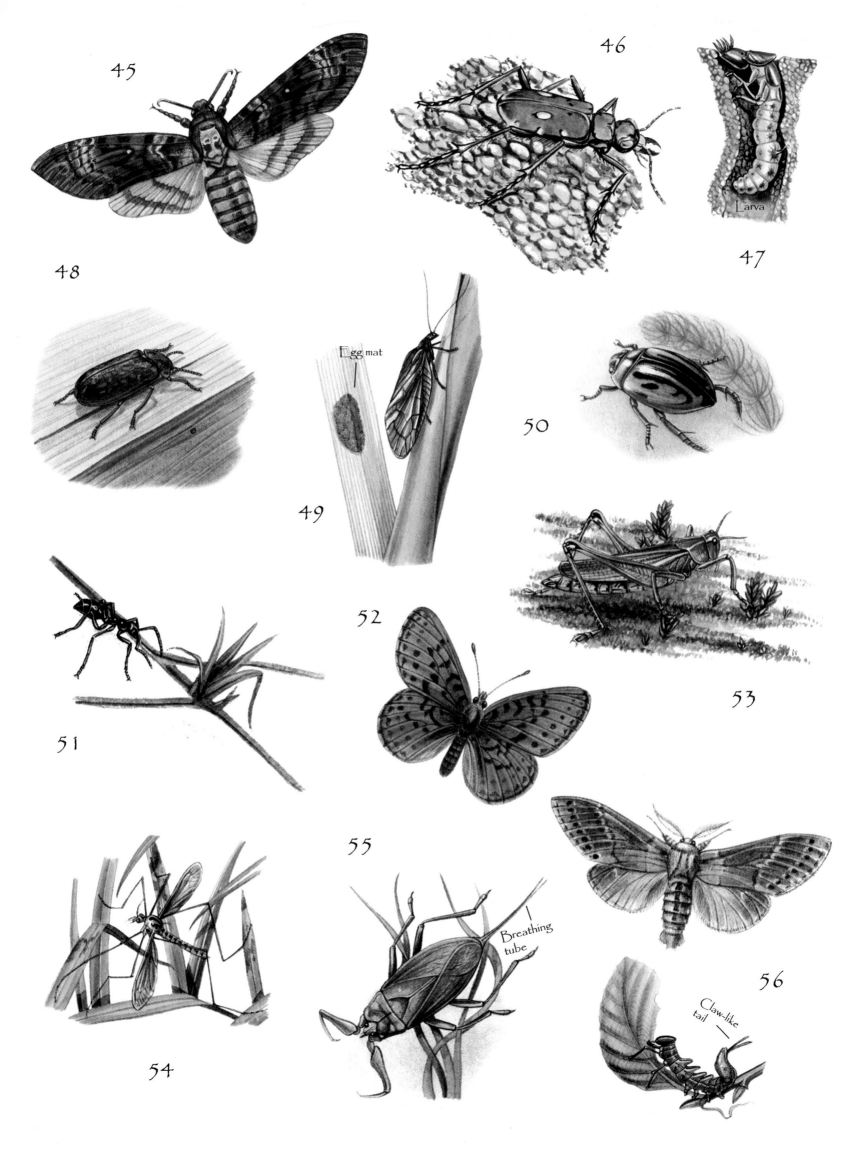

45

46

47

Larva

48

49

Egg mat

50

51

52

53

54

55

Breathing tube

56

Claw-like tail

57

60 ♂

58 ♀

59

61

63 ♀

62

64 ♂

66

Garden tiger

Woolly bear

Larva

65

67

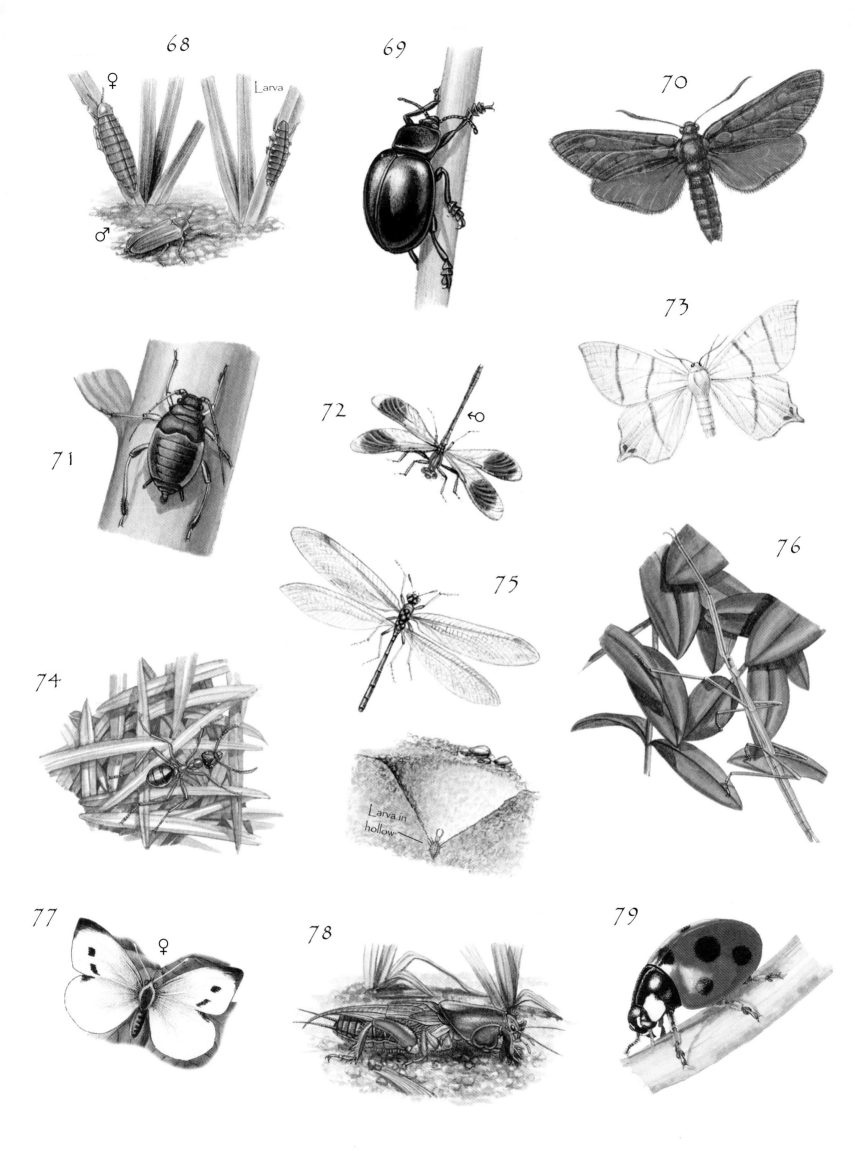

68
♀
Larva
♂

69

70

71

72
♂

73

74

75
Larva in
hollow

76

77
♀

78

79

80

81

82

83

84

85

♂

Larva

86

87

88

89

90

91

Larva

92

93

94

95

96

97

Lappet

98

99

100

101

102

103

104

105

106

107

108

109 ♀

110

111

112

Rose aphid or greenfly

Length: 2–3mm

A rose aphid, or greenfly, is green or pinkish and shaped like a bulb. Its antennae are long compared to its body. This bug feeds on roses in the spring, making itself a pest. It produces a sweet, sticky syrup called honeydew, which ants eat.

WHEN ....

WHERE ....

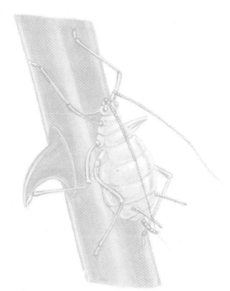
Rose aphid

Black bean aphid or blackfly

Length: 2–3mm

Broad beans and thistles often house large groups (called colonies) of these tiny, black bugs living together.

WHEN ....

WHERE ....

Green shieldbug

Length: 12–14mm

You might find green shieldbugs on trees such as hazel and birch. They have a broad, green body with a light brown abdomen and beady antennae.

WHEN ....

WHERE ....

Black bean aphid

Green shieldbug

Green leafhopper

Length: 6–9mm

This bug has a long, straight green body with brown legs. It is common all over Britain and feeds on grasses and rushes.

WHEN ....

WHERE ....

Green leafhopper

Breathing tube

Water scorpion

Water scorpion

Length: 18–22mm

Water scorpions have claw-like front legs which they use to catch small fish, tadpoles and insect larvae. They have brown bodies with a long breathing tube sticking out behind.

WHEN ....

WHERE ....

Dragonflies, Damselflies

Broad-bodied chaser

Wingspan: 75mm

Male broad-bodied chasers have broad, pale blue bodies with yellow markings. Females are brown with yellow markings. They are very common in southern England.

WHEN ....

WHERE ....

Broad-bodied chaser

Downy emerald

Downy emerald

Wingspan: 68mm

This dragonfly has a bright green body and see-through wings.

WHEN ....

WHERE ....

Blue-tailed damselfly

Wingspan: 35mm

Blue-tailed damselfly

The blue tip of its long abdomen gives this clear-winged dragonfly its name. It can be found resting on plants in wet areas.

WHEN ....

WHERE ....

Ruddy darter

Wingspan: 55mm

You can find ruddy darters around weedy ponds or ditches in marshy areas, but they are getting rarer. They have golden-brown bodies and see-through wings.

WHEN ....

WHERE ....

Ruddy darter

Banded demoiselle

Wingspan: 60–65mm

Males have a blue body and bright blue flashes on each wing, while females are green with see-through green wings.

WHEN ....

WHERE ....

Beautiful demoiselle

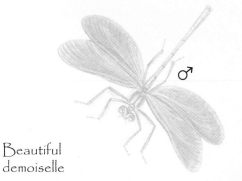

Beautiful demoiselle

Wingspan: 58–63mm

Beautiful demoiselles have green bodies and wings with long, thick veins. The females have golden-brown wings.

WHEN ....

WHERE ....

Banded demoiselle

Bees, Wasps

Red-tailed bumblebee

Length: 22mm

Often found in gardens, this bee has a big, black, furry body with an orange-red tip. The queen makes her nest in a hole in the ground.

WHEN ....

WHERE ....

Red-tailed bumblebee

Potter wasp

Male length: 12mm
Female length: 14mm

Potter wasps make small clay pots for their larvae. They then fill the pots with little caterpillars which they paralyse with their sting.

WHEN ....

WHERE ....

Potter wasp

Pot

Sand wasp

Length: 28–30mm

These wasps capture caterpillars, paralyse them with their stings, then bury them in burrows in the sand. Their larvae feed on them as they grow. There are various types of sand wasp. This one has a long, skinny orange abdomen with a bulb-shaped tip.

WHEN ....

WHERE ....

Sand wasp

Ruby-tailed wasp

Ruby-tailed wasp

Length: 12mm

This wasp is also known as a cuckoo wasp. This is because, just as a cuckoo lays its eggs in the nest of another bird, the female lays her egg in the nest of another wasp, or bee. The wasp larva then eats that insect's food, egg or larva.

WHEN ....

WHERE ....

Leaf-cutter bee

Leaf-cutter bee

Male length: 10mm
Female length: 11mm

Leaf-cutter bees cut semi-circular pieces from rose leaves to make cylinders where females lay a single egg. They store these cylinders in hollow stems and dead wood.

WHEN ....

WHERE ....

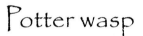

15

Wasps

Oak marble gall-wasp

Length: 4mm

This wasp has a small, reddish-brown body and grey wings. It lays its egg in a leaf bud, and as the larva feeds, the tree forms a solid lump, or gall, around it.

WHEN ....

WHERE ....

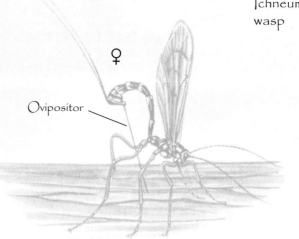

Ichneumon wasp

♀

Ovipositor

Marble gall

Oak marble gall-wasp

Ichneumon wasp

Length: 22–30mm

These are large wasps with long legs. The females have a thin tube, called an ovipositor, which is longer than their body. They use it to pierce holes in pine trees and to lay their eggs inside them.

WHEN ....

WHERE ....

Hornet

Length: 22–30mm

Hornet

Hornets are very large with brown and yellow markings on their abdomens.

WHEN ....

WHERE ....

German wasp

Length: 15–20mm

German wasps are very common in Britain. They build paper nests, sometimes in attics, or gaps in stonework.

WHEN ....

WHERE ....

Velvet ant

♀

Velvet ant

Length: 15mm

These are not ants, but wasps. They are named for the females, which are wingless and ant-like. They have a rounded, red thorax and a black abdomen marked with a light ring and four light flecks.

WHEN ....

WHERE ....

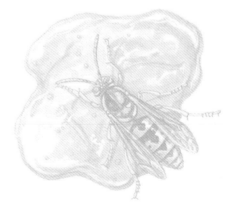

German wasp

Wasps, Sawfly, Ants

Horntail or giant wood wasp

Length: 25–32mm

Horntails are large, black and hairy, with yellow stripes on their abdomens and yellow pads behind their eyes. Their larvae feed on dead wood and fungus.

WHEN ....

WHERE ....

Horntail

♀

Wood ant

Wood ant

Length: 5–11mm

The largest ants in Britain, these live in woods, where they make large, conical nests from twigs and leaves or pine needles. They can't sting, but they do bite enemies then spray acid at them.

WHEN ....

WHERE ....

Birch sawfly

Length: 20–23mm

These sawflies have a dark body with a small, yellow fleck around the top of their abdomen. Their larvae have three pairs of true legs and six pairs of stubby, unjointed legs called prolegs.

WHEN ....

WHERE ....

Birch sawfly

Blue horntail

Length: 20–25mm

Female blue horntails are a deep metallic blue. The males have a blue head, thorax and tail-end, with a yellow abdomen. They live in pine forests.

WHEN ....

WHERE ....

Black ant

Black ant

Length: 3–9mm

These ants are black, and common in gardens. The males die after mating, and the queens then start new nests, or colonies, on their own.

WHEN ....

WHERE ....

Blue horntail

♀

True flies

Hover fly

Grey flesh fly

Length: 6–17mm

Grey flesh flies have black and grey markings on their body, and reddish-brown eyes. They are common, and lay their eggs in the rotting flesh of dead animals.

WHEN ....

WHERE ....

Grey flesh fly

Hover fly

Length: 10–14mm

There are many types of hover fly. This one is brown, with three light stripes on each side of its abdomen. Hover flies look a bit like wasps, but do not sting.

WHEN ....

WHERE ....

Horse fly

Length: 20–25mm

A loud hum warns that a female horse fly is about to bite. Horse flies have dark brown bodies, and each section of the abdomen has light brown edges. They have large, green eyes.

WHEN ....

WHERE ....

Dung fly

Length: 10–12mm

You can find dung flies around fresh cowpats, where the females lay their eggs. This kind has a bright golden body. When dung flies are disturbed, they rise in a buzzing mass, but soon settle again.

WHEN ....

WHERE ....

Horse fly

Dung fly

Greenbottle fly

Length: 7–11mm

This fly is bright green and can be found among flowers. Most types of greenbottle lay their eggs in or on dead animals.

WHEN ....

WHERE ....

Greenbottle fly

True flies, Ant-lion

Giant cranefly or daddy-long-legs

Length: 30–40mm

This large fly has a long, spindly body and very long legs. It is often found near water. Its larvae are called leatherjackets, and they eat root crops and grass roots.

WHEN ....

WHERE ....

Leatherjacket

Giant cranefly

Ant-lion

Ant-lion

Length: 35mm

Ant-lions are long, with four broad, white wings. Their larvae trap ants and other insects in sandy hollows and then suck them dry. Ant-lions are common in southern Europe.

WHEN ....

WHERE ....

Tiger cranefly

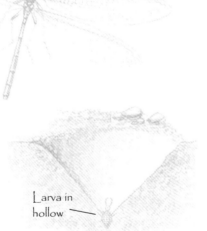

Larva in hollow

Tiger cranefly

Length: 18–20mm

This cranefly has a long, yellow body with black markings, and very long, thin legs.

WHEN ....

WHERE ....

Bee fly

Length: 10–11mm

Bee flies have round, furry bodies, and fly around garden flowers looking for nectar in early spring. They are most common in southern England.

WHEN ....

WHERE ....

Bee fly

Common gnat or mosquito

Length: 6–7mm

A common gnat is small, with a golden-brown body and very long, thin legs. The female sucks blood from people and animals.

WHEN ....

WHERE ....

Common gnat

Lacy-winged insects, Scorpion fly

Lacewings, snake flies and alder flies all have wings with fine, delicately patterned veins.

Giant lacewing

Length: 15mm

You are most likely to spot a giant lacewing at night. It has very long, wavy antennae and large, see-through wings covered in brown, lace-like veins.

WHEN ....

WHERE ....

Scorpion fly

♂ Curly tail

♀

Scorpion fly

Length: 18–22mm

Scorpion flies are named because of the male's scorpion-like tail. They eat dead insects, often stolen from spiders' webs.

WHEN ....

WHERE ....

Snake fly

Giant lacewing

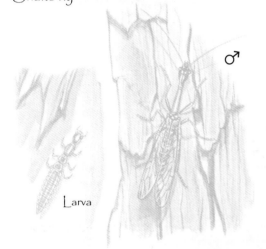

♂

Larva

Green lacewing

Length: 15mm

Green lacewings have four wings covered with green, lace-like veins. You can find them mainly around gardens and hedges.

WHEN ....

WHERE ....

Egg mat

Alder fly

Snake fly

Length: 15–20mm

Snake flies are so called because of the cobra-like way they bend their heads and thoraxes. They have a long head and thorax and thin, see-through wings. They are often found on oak trees.

WHEN ....

WHERE ....

Alder fly

Length: 20mm

An alder fly lays its eggs in mats on the stems of water plants. It flies in a slow, heavy way. This type of alder fly has large, brownish wings and long antennae.

WHEN ....

WHERE ....

Green lacewing

Mayfly, Stonefly, Crickets

Mayfly

Mayfly

Length: 40mm

Adult mayflies do not live long – sometimes just for a few hours. Their nymphs live in ponds and streams. This large mayfly has long tails and see-through, brown-striped wings.

WHEN ....

WHERE ....

Stonefly

Stonefly

Length: 22mm

Stoneflies have long, overlapping wings. Their nymphs have long tails and live on riverbeds, feeding on other small animals.

WHEN ....

WHERE ....

House cricket

Length: 16mm

You may hear a house cricket's shrill song in and around heated buildings and greenhouses in winter. They are also found in rubbish heaps.

WHEN ....

WHERE ....

House cricket

Mole cricket

Length: 38–42mm

This large, extremely rare cricket has front feet shaped like spades, which it uses for digging. The outside of its thorax grows forwards over its head, looking like an armour case. The male has a long, whirring call.

WHEN ....

WHERE ....

Mole cricket

Field cricket

Length: 20mm

Field crickets are very rare. They have black bodies and legs, long antennae and brown wing cases. The males "sing" by rubbing their wing cases together, to attract females.

WHEN ....

WHERE ....

Field cricket

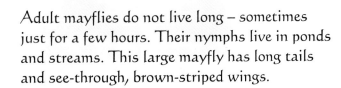

Bush crickets, Grasshopper, Stick insect

Great green bush cricket

Length: 45–47mm

Great green bush crickets have long wings and antennae, and long, thin back legs. They make a loud, shrill noise, move slowly and never fly very far.

WHEN ....

WHERE ....

Great green bush cricket

Wart-biter

Length: 34–35mm

A wart-biter looks a lot like a great green bush cricket, but smaller, with shorter antennae and dark markings on its green wings. It may bite when it is handled. People in Sweden used to use this insect to bite off their warts.

WHEN ....

WHERE ....

Wart-biter

Stick insect

Length: up to 90mm

These insects are so-called because their very long, thin, green bodies look like sticks with spindly legs attached. They do not live in Britain, except for a small number in the southwest. A similar type, called the laboratory stick insect, is often kept as a pet.

WHEN ....

WHERE ....

Stick insect

Large marsh grasshopper

Length: 27–32mm

Found only in boggy areas, these grasshoppers have yellow and black abdomens, red and brown heads and thoraxes, short antennae and long back legs. The male has a slow, ticking song and, when it flies, its wings look silvery.

WHEN ....

WHERE ....

Large marsh grasshopper

Praying mantis, Cockroaches, Earwig

Praying mantis

Length: 60–80mm

A praying mantis has a long, green body, with a small head and large front legs. It holds these together, as if praying, while it waits to catch insects. It is found in southern Europe.

WHEN ....

WHERE ....

Praying mantis

Dusky cockroach

Length: 7–10mm

Unlike most cockroaches, this small insect lives outside. It looks very like a German cockroach (see below) but, as its name suggests, is darker in colour.

WHEN ....

WHERE ....

Common cockroach

Length: 25mm

Often seen as pests, as they come into houses for warmth, these insects are large, black to brown and shiny, with spiny legs and long antennae. Their heads are covered by the front of the thorax, like a helmet.

WHEN ....

WHERE ....

German cockroach

Length: 13mm

Despite their name, German cockroaches probably come from north Africa or the Middle East. They have a light brown body with two dark streaks on their head, and long, folded wing cases.

WHEN ....

WHERE ....

Dusky cockroach

Common cockroach

Common earwig

Length: 15mm

Common earwigs are brown, and have tiny wing cases and long abdomens with pincers at the end. When they feel threatened, they spread and raise their pincers. They can fly, but don't often do so.

WHEN ....

WHERE ....

German cockroach

Common earwig

♂

Index and checklist

This list will help you find every insect in the book. The first number after each insect tells you which page it's on. The second number is the number of the sticker.

Digital imaging by Will Dawes
Cover image © Oswald Eckstein/zefa/Corbis; Back cover image © D. Hurst/Alamy
This edition first published in 2007 by Usborne Publishing Ltd, Usborne House, 83–85 Saffron Hill, London EC1N 8RT, England.
www.usborne.com © 2007, 2001, 1997, 1994, 1986, 1979 Usborne Publishing Ltd. The name Usborne and the devices ♀ ⊕ are
Trade Marks of Usborne Publishing Ltd.